Ben Raskin

COMPOST

a family guide to making soil from scraps

Leaping Hare Press

First published in the UK in 2013 by

Leaping Hare Press

210 High Street, Lewes

East Sussex BN7 2NS

United Kingdom

www.leapingharepress.co.uk

British Library Cataloguing-in-Publication Data
A catalogue record for this book is available
from the British Library

ISBN: 978-1-78240-048-6

This book was conceived, designed & produced by

Leaping Hare Press

Creative Director PETER BRIDGEWATER
Publisher SUSAN KELLY
Commissioning Editor MONICA PERDONI
Art Director WAYNE BLADES
Senior Editor JACQUI SAYERS
Designer CLARE BARBER
Illustrator TONWEN JONES

Printed in China
Colour origination by Ivy Press Reprographics

Distributed worldwide (except North America)
by Thames & Hudson Ltd., 181A High Holborn,
London WC1V 7QX, United Kingdom

10 9 8 7 6 5 4 3 2 1

Contents

Introduction

All fruit and vegetables rot – just try leaving a banana on the windowsill in the sun for a few days and see what happens! Rotting is nature's way of recycling the goodness – known as nutrients – found in plants, so it can be used to help new plants to grow, which in turn helps animals to live. The picture opposite shows how this cycle of nutrients works.

All 'organic matter' – that means any plant or animal, living or dead – rots down into something called 'humus'. That's not the tasty hummus you might have eaten, though! This sort of humus is rich, brown, sticky stuff, and it's full of nutrients. Some things take much longer to break down into humus than others and, although we know how some of this happens, even scientists don't fully understand how humus is made. What we do know is that it is great for our soil and our plants!

In this book we will look at how composting works, some of the animals and organisms that make it happen, and how you can get started on making and using your own compost.

POOP ROTS DOWN
to compost, feeding
the new grass for the
cows to eat.

HOW IT WORKS

COWS EAT GRASS
and lots of it, all
through their lives.

OOPS!

BIRDS POOP
onto grass, and
their poop is full
of goodness.

WE EAT COWS
(or at least if we're not
vegetarians we do.)

BIRDS EAT WORMS ...
and plenty of them!

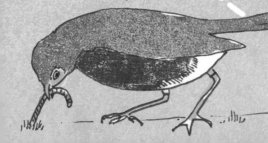

WORMS EAT US,
but don't worry, it only
happens after we die!

what is compost?

Our everyday word for rotted down stuff (humus) is 'compost', and compost is the best thing ever to help new plants to grow. As we don't want piles of smelly veggie leftovers rotting in the kitchen, we use compost bins or heaps. If you look after your leftovers as they rot, you will be rewarded with heaps of lovely compost!

Compost in nature

You don't see compost heaps in nature. This is because organic matter lands all over the place, bit by bit. Leaves fall from trees, animals go to the toilet, and plants and animals (**organisms**) die. What happens to all of this organic matter? It doesn't just pile up and sit there forever, does it? The answer is that everything, living or dead, has

something else that will eat it. This is often called a 'food chain' – though this makes it sound like it is happening in one direction but it really all goes on in a big circle.

For instance, in a forest, juicy nuts that fall to the ground will be eaten by animals like squirrels. The poo from the squirrel, and its whole body when it dies, becomes food for the worms, fungi and **microorganisms** in the soil. Once they have eaten and broken down the material, the nutrients are released, and the trees can use these to grow and produce more nuts. So all plants and animals are broken down, and the goodness is taken up by other living things in a 'circle of life'.

An '**organism**' is an animal, plant, or single-celled life form – anything that is living.

SOCIETY RULES

I promise to:

* Always be kind to worms

* Make compost and put it on our garden

* Look after soil

* Not mind too much if the birds eat some worms (they need to live too)

* Tell all my friends about how great worms are

Why not show your dedication to the Society by displaying a photo of your favourite worm in the frame overleaf?

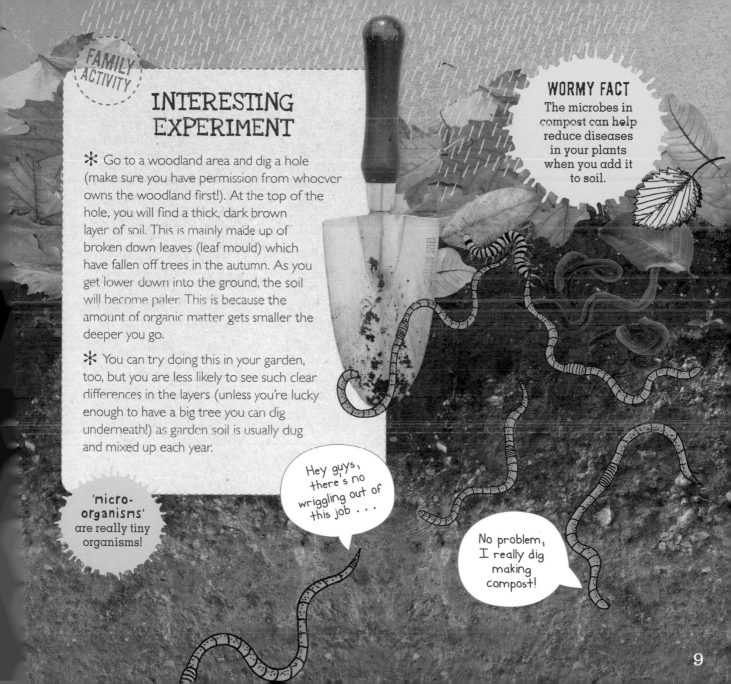

INTERESTING EXPERIMENT

✳ Go to a woodland area and dig a hole (make sure you have permission from whoever owns the woodland first!). At the top of the hole, you will find a thick, dark brown layer of soil. This is mainly made up of broken down leaves (leaf mould) which have fallen off trees in the autumn. As you get lower down into the ground, the soil will become paler. This is because the amount of organic matter gets smaller the deeper you go.

✳ You can try doing this in your garden, too, but you are less likely to see such clear differences in the layers (unless you're lucky enough to have a big tree you can dig underneath!) as garden soil is usually dug and mixed up each year.

WORMY FACT
The microbes in compost can help reduce diseases in your plants when you add it to soil.

'micro-organisms' are really tiny organisms!

Hey guys, there's no wriggling out of this job . . .

No problem, I really dig making compost!

How to copy nature

Making compost at home is basically just copying what happens in nature. All the ingredients that we need – water, air, organisms – are all around, we just need to provide the right conditions for them to work in a way that fits our allotment, garden, balcony or windowsill.

If we really copied nature, then we would just spread all of our rotting fruit and veg in a thin layer over the ground and wait for it to be taken down into the soil. This is sometimes called 'scatter composting'. It does have some advantages – it's quick and easy and you don't have to worry about looking after a compost heap. But who likes to look at lots of half rotten veg in their garden? This is also more likely to attract unwanted guests, like rats and foxes, to the garden.

DIG AND DROP

Dig and drop

Another simple way to let nature do most of the work for you is to put your veg waste into a hole in the ground. This method is called **dig-and-drop**. To do this you dig a hole, fill it up with your veg and garden waste (ideally layering brown and green material as you would in a normal compost heap – see page 37), then cover it all over with soil.

SCATTER COMPOSTING

Munch

Munch

All the waste material rots down in the hole and benefits the soil. This is quick and easy, but only one bit of your garden gets the goodness from the nutrients. You can of course dig the hole in a new place each time, to spread the benefit. This method can work well in a veg garden but is trickier in a flower garden where there are lots of plants with roots you don't want to disturb.

> I'm going in blind, but that's no problem!

> Easy peasy, I smell lemon peel squeazy!

Heaps and bins

Most people prefer to have more control over the composting process, so make a heap or use a container, such as a special compost bin, that can be covered with something, such as a wooden lid or piece of old carpet. These options allow you to keep the compost in one place and spread its goodness around your garden once it has rotted down. We will look at how to do this a bit later on pages 30 and 31.

WORMY FACT
Although worms don't have eyes, they can detect light and will move away from it.

11

What is Soil?

You may think that soil is just the dirt that gets stuck on your shoes when you've been outside, but there is a lot more to it than that. Soil is a mixture of different minerals, organic matter, water and air. If it is healthy it will also be bustling with life – some things you can see, like worms, and some that you would need a microscope to see.

Types of soil

Soil can be divided into different types, according to its 'texture'. This describes the size of the mineral particles that the soil is actually made of. The three main types of soil are sand, silt and clay.

Most soils are a mixture of these types, and there is a complicated way that soil scientists work out exactly what kind of soil you have, depending on the amount of each one.

✳ Sand has the biggest mineral particles, which measure between 0.05mm and 2mm – that is really, really small, but the other two types are even smaller!

✳ Silt particles measure a tiny 0.002mm to 0.05mm and would only just be visible if you had one on your finger.

✳ Clay particles are the smallest of all, and you'd need a microscope to see them – they are the bits in soil that are smaller than 0.002mm.

Complexity of soil

You could say that we know more about the moon than we do about what goes on under our feet in the soil. With billions of organisms in every spadeful, we only understand a bit of what is going on at a microscopic level in a healthy living soil. There are tiny tunnels, homes, families of organisms and great clusters of activity.

Think of a big city like London or New York, and everything that happens there every day. People eat, talk, fight, laugh, cry... Shrink all of that down so that it fits into a bucket and you can start to picture what is happening down there in the soil.

Toot toot! We have places to be and compost to make!

Out of the way, burrow hog!

WORMY FACT
A desert has no topsoil, while in rainforests such as the Amazon, the topsoil is up to 10 metres deep!

How is soil made?

Soil is made as rock breaks down into smaller and smaller pieces and gets mixed with organic matter. This usually happens very slowly over many thousands of years. There are lots of ways that big pieces of rock can become smaller. Here are just a couple:

GLACIERS – huge rivers of ice that move slowly down across continents, taking large boulders and grinding them up as they move. When the ice melts, these smaller pieces of rock are left behind to form part of the soil.

ICE – many types of rock are porous. This means they can absorb water. If they are very wet and it gets cold, the water inside them freezes and turns to ice. Ice takes up more space than water and when it expands it shatters the rock into smaller pieces.

There are lots of other processes that bring things into soil as well. For instance, if a river floods it washes mineral particles onto the soil that stay there when the flooding goes down again. Some minerals will also dissolve in rain. Sometimes the wind can blow volcanic dust or sand from a desert across the world and that will get mixed into the soil when it falls.

Let's worm our way in...

WORMY FACT

Herbivores eat only plants. Predators eat other animals – if they only eat animals they are carnivores, but if they also eat plants, they are omnivores.

ACID AND ALKALINE SOIL

All soils are either acid or alkaline, depending on the type of rock the soil is made from. This is measured using a scale from 0 to 14, called 'pH' – pH7 is neutral, less than 7 is acidic and more than 7 is alkaline. The pH can affect which plants can grow in your soil.

   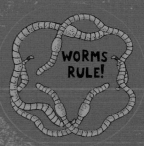

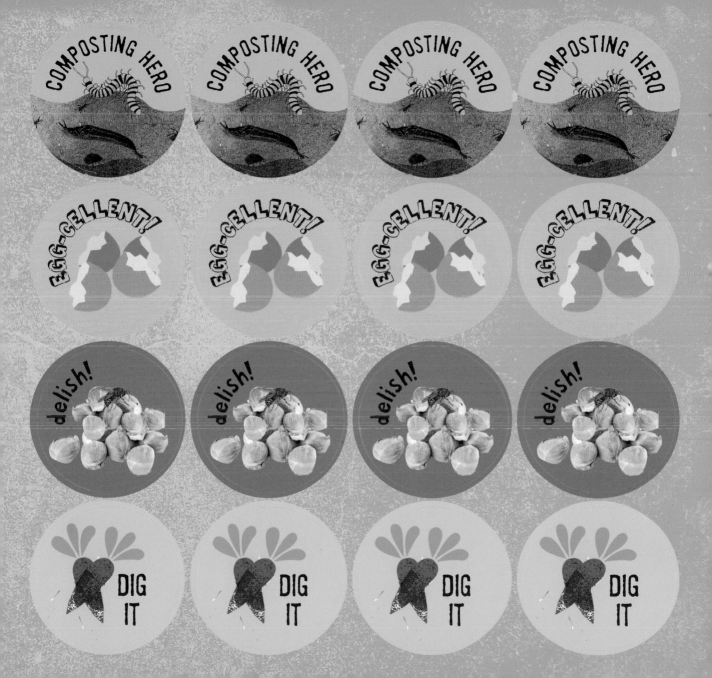

What lives in soil?

Many thousands of different organisms live in soil, so we can only peek at some of the commonest ones here. If you can get your hands on a microscope then maybe you could see some of these really close up, but even a magnifying glass will help!

FUNGI Not just mushrooms or toadstools! Below ground, the fungus has a root-like structure called a 'mycelium' which can be miles long.

WORMS These giant herbivores of the soil don't interact much with the rest of the soil life until they die and become food for it.

WORMY FACT
There are likely to be at least 100 million bacteria in one teaspoon of soil.

ALGAE Cousins to bacteria – they come in many colours such as green, red and brown. Like plants, they can use sunlight to make their own food (this is called photosynthesis).

BACTERIA Tiny microorganisms vital to human and plant life. We often hear about bad bacteria, but there are many good bacteria that help us to stay healthy – lots of them even live inside us!

ARCHAEA Like bacteria, but able to take nitrogen from the air (often called 'fixing') and make it available to plants. They can live in extreme temperatures.

PROTOZOA Bigger and more complicated than bacteria (which they often eat) – they also eat nematodes.

CENTIPEDES These are long, thin predators with lots of legs. They lay their eggs in soil and rely on other soil organisms for food.

NEMATODES Tiny worm-like creatures that mostly eat bacteria and fungus. They are hard to see without a microscope!

15

How compost helps soil

A soil with no compost, or organic matter, is a dead soil. Imagine a town with no shops to buy food – no one would want to live there! Compost provides lots of nutritious food not only for the plants we want to grow, but also for the tiny organisms that live in the soil.

Nutrients

What's really clever about compost and all the tasty goodies inside it is that it holds all of this food in a stable way. This means that it becomes available slowly, rather than all being ready at once.

This should keep me going for a month or two...

Imagine having to eat all the meals you needed for a whole month at once – you might be able to eat a few, but soon you would be too full and the rest would have to be thrown away! Well, plants are the same – they need food most of the year round and compost is nature's way of preserving food, and keeping it ready until it is needed.

Like eating a balanced meal, getting the balance of nutrients right is also really important. A bowl of soup with just potatoes in it would be boring and wouldn't give you all the vitamins and protein that you need to stay healthy. A good compost will have a wide range of nutrients to add to what is available from the mineral part of the soil.

ESSENTIAL NUTRIENTS

Here are some of the most important nutrients that soil life and plants need in order to survive:

NITROGEN Plants need more of this than any other nutrient to grow well (but too much can make a plant floppy and more likely to get a disease). Nitrogen dissolves very easily in water, which means it can get washed away, so getting lots of organic matter into your soil really helps hang on to it.

PHOSPHORUS This is very important for making flowers and fruits.

POTASSIUM This is great for root development.

SULPHUR Good for seed development, and also helps plants resist disease and pests.

CALCIUM This is needed when the plant is growing, and also affects the pH (see page 14) of the soil.

MAGNESIUM Plants need this for making chlorophyll – which is what makes them green.

WORMY FACT
A 5 per cent increase in organic material can increase soil's ability to hold water by four times.

Structure

Earlier we looked at the different types of soil texture (see page 12). The soil 'structure' describes how those bits are held together. You will know that on a beach, sand doesn't hold together at all and water just runs through it. This is the same for sandy soil, but if you add lots of compost to it then it clumps together, and starts to absorb some water.

In clay soil, the opposite is true – pure clay is very solid and holds lots of water. When it dries out it forms a solid lump, but mixing in compost breaks it up, making the soil more crumbly and helping drainage.

Water

When it's really hot, soils can dry out, and when this happens a lot of the creatures in the soil either die or have to dig down to deeper levels to wait for better weather. Plants need water to survive, too, and trying to grow them when there is no rain can be very difficult. Clay soils can end up as solid as a brick in this sort of weather, which plants really don't like.

WORMY FACT
One acre of soil can be home to up to 10 tonnes of living creatures.

WITHOUT ORGANIC MATTER

WITH ORGANIC MATTER

Although we need some rain, if it rains all the time then soil can get too wet. This means that many organisms in the soil can drown, and plant roots can't breathe either.

Adding compost to your soil can help in both hot, dry and cold, wet weather. Because compost holds on to water well, it stops light (sandy) soils drying out so quickly. And on heavier (clay) soils, adding compost opens the structure, allowing it to drain more quickly and letting air into the soil so that plants and animals can breathe.

DRAINAGE PROBLEMS

Not having enough organic matter, or compost, in your soil can cause problems such as a thin, hard layer developing on the surface of the soil. This stops water from getting into the soil and means it just runs away. This can make it hard for seeds to germinate but can also lead to your soil and its nutrients being washed away, so getting plenty of organic matter into your soil really is important!

My favourite soil is light and fluffy, like a delicious sponge cake...

Mudcake is my favourite!

WORMY FACT
Most soil contains between 2 and 5 per cent organic matter. Rich, peaty soils (found in bogs) can have more than 20 per cent, while soils that have been farmed a lot without any organic matter being added can have as little as 1 per cent.

Worms galore!

There are lots of types of worm, but we are interested in earthworms. You've probably seen them wriggling around in soil and, to be honest, they don't look that special. But don't be deceived by their looks! Worms are amazing and they are the stars of the composting show.

What do worms do?

Worms eat soil and organic matter – up to one third of their body weight every day! They take a little bit of it as food but most of it passes through them in a slightly broken down form. The organic matter in the soil is the part they use as food.

Breaking down the other stuff helps other organisms that prefer their compost in smaller bits. Have you seen the tiny piles of earth called 'casts' that worms leave on the surface of grass? This is worm poo (though it is mostly made up of soil). If you pick it up, you'll feel that it's crumbly, without any big lumps in it. It's full of good nutrients.

Worms also dig burrows into the soil. Different species dig to different depths, and some dig sideways and some dig downwards. This means that in a healthy soil there will be a maze of tunnels. These tunnels help in lots of ways, for instance helping water to drain out after heavy rain, and allowing oxygen to get deeper into the soil. Most of the creatures we want in the soil need oxygen to breathe, so this is really important.

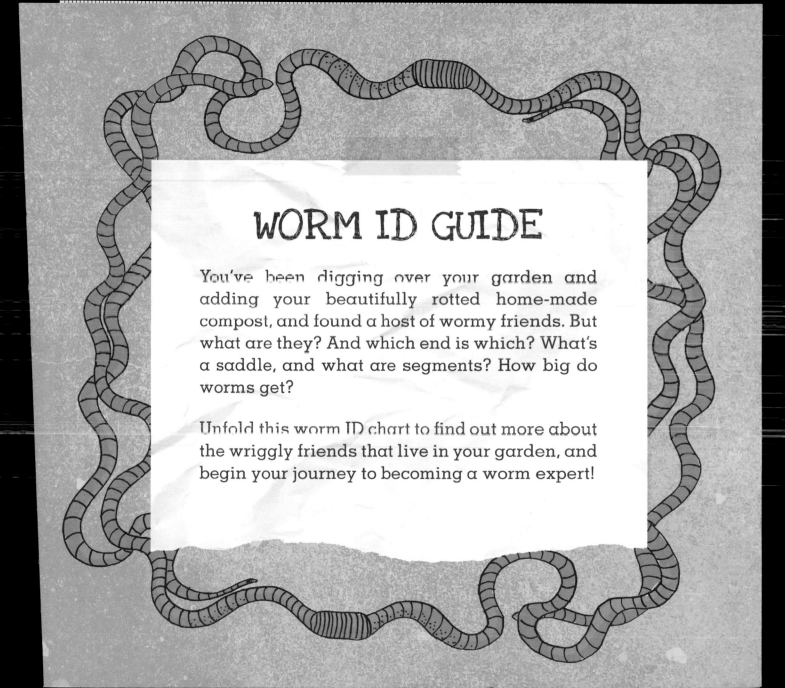

WORM ID GUIDE

You've been digging over your garden and adding your beautifully rotted home-made compost, and found a host of wormy friends. But what are they? And which end is which? What's a saddle, and what are segments? How big do worms get?

Unfold this worm ID chart to find out more about the wriggly friends that live in your garden, and begin your journey to becoming a worm expert!

NOTES

You can use this page to keep a record of the size and colour of the worms you find.

Who's who?

There are thought to be thousands of different species of earthworms in the world. Some of them are quite rare and many species have moved around the world with human settlers. Some species may be found only in glasshouses or other 'unnatural' places, and couldn't survive in normal soil.

There are a few types of earthworm that make their home under rotting tree bark, or even in semi-aquatic (watery) conditions, but mostly they do as their name suggests and live in the soil. You can divide worms into three groups depending on which part of the soil they live in – the surface, the topsoil or the subsoil. See if you can find them all!

SURFACE WORMS These like very rich soil with lots of organic matter and tend to be small and dark in colour (which helps with camouflage from predators). The brandling worm (*Eisenia fetida*) is one of these, and it can't even survive in the soil as it needs a really rich habitat. You can find them in piles of old leaves and rotten wood, or in your compost heap or bin.

TOPSOIL WORMS

Worms that like to live in the topsoil (usually down to about 20cm in depth) are the most common. They eat lots and tend to have shallow horizontal burrows. If you go digging in your garden you are quite likely to find some of these worms.

SUBSOIL WORMS Worms that live in the subsoil (under the topsoil) usually have a permanent burrow, which can be up to 3 metres deep! They still need to come up to the surface layers of the soil to feed though, so you might find them if you look.

LATIN NAMES

Latin names are used in science to precisely describe plants and animals, according to which groups they belong to. The same species may have different common names (like brandling worm, red wiggler, or compost worm), but the same Latin name (*Eisenia fetida*) is used around the world, helping to avoid confusion!

WORMS LOVE

LOTS OF FOOD! This is why it's so important to keep feeding the soil with compost.

MOIST, WARM SOIL Although they can survive extremes by going into a form of hibernation, they prefer it when the soil is neither too wet nor too cold or too dry.

BEING UNDISTURBED The best habitat for a worm is permanent cover, allowing it to build its burrows and breed happily.

I LOVE worms!

WORMS HATE

WATERLOGGED SOIL In very wet weather, if the ground is underwater for days at a time, then many worms will drown.

REALLY DRY SOIL Worms will burrow down deep to get to moist soil and in very extreme conditions curl themselves into a tight ball and wait for rain.

BEING CUT IN HALF! There is a myth that if you cut a worm in half you get two worms. Unfortunately, this isn't true. They can survive being cut if you miss their vital organs, but they certainly don't multiply.

I'm getting out of my depth here.

Who eats worms?

Worms are made up of about 70 per cent protein. This means lots of things like to eat them!

• All kinds of birds such as blackbirds and robins
• Mammals such as moles, hedgehogs, badgers and foxes
• Carnivorous snails
• Man – we don't usually eat them, but sometimes our spades and ploughs do! **whoops!**

Learning from worms

Identifying which types of worm you have in your soil can help you understand more about it. Using the fold-out worm measuring chart in this book could help you recognize who's who in your garden, and tell you more about what's going on underground…

If you can find the big **lob worm** (*Lumbricus terrestris*) in your soil, then you are probably looking after it well – this worm really likes rich soils with lots of organic matter. It comes out at night.

The **grey worm** (*Allolobophora caliginosa*) tends to like poorer soils, so it this is the main one you find then you probably should be adding a bit more compost or manure to your garden.

If you've got the **black-headed worm** (*Aporrectodea longa*), then you almost certainly have an alkaline soil. This worm is quite large and can make worm casts of more than 5cm tall.

Brandling worms (*Eisenia fetida*) need lots of organic matter, which is why they love the compost heap so much. They don't normally survive in soil unless it is really rich.

One of the commonest worms is the **green worm** (*Allolobophora chlorotica*). It doesn't like very acidic soils, though it can cope with slightly acidic ones. Despite its name, it can be a pale grey colour. If you touch it, it can ooze out lots of yellow liquid!

BAD WORMS

Not all worms are good – there are some that eat other worms! In Europe, some species of flatworm have invaded from Australia and New Zealand and are eating up earthworms, while in America there are 'hammerhead worms' doing the same.

WORMY FACT
Charles Darwin called worms 'nature's ploughs' because they bring organic matter from the surface down into different depths of the soil.

Compost friends

It's not just worms that break down organic matter. There are billions of organisms working away – some of them are similar to those that live in the soil (see page 15). They all have a job to do and, like any good team, they have different skills, which are needed at different stages of the composting process.

Bacteria

Usually around 80–90 per cent of the organisms living in compost are bacteria, and they do the most work.

Actinomycetes

These are a cleverer group of bacteria that form little threads. If you sniff some good compost, it should smell a bit earthy; this smell comes from the actinomycetes. They are good at breaking down the tougher stuff like cardboard, twiggy stems or tree bark.

Fungi

These tackle the really heavy jobs in composting, particularly woody material, and often prepare the material ready for bacteria to finish their work. Although they do work at all stages of the composting process, they don't like it when it gets really hot and tend to escape to the cooler edges of the compost.

CREEPY CRAWLIES

BUGS

FUNGI

'biodiversity' means the range of types of life in a place. The more plant and animal species that you have living in your garden, the more biodiverse it is.

COMPOST BINGO

COMPOST BINGO

This card turns making great compost into a fun game!

It works best with more than one player – you can photocopy or scan this card and give a copy to a friend, then see who can complete it first.

1 Hunt around your home and garden and see how many of the items that are pictured overleaf you can find, then tick them off the card as you add them to your compost. You might find lots all at once, or you might have to wait for some things. You could put stickers on things that aren't ready yet, so you don't forget.

2 For each line (horizontal or vertical) that you tick off, give yourself a 'composting hero' or 'champion!' sticker.

3 Once you have ticked off everything on the card, the game is finished – Bingo! – and you can even add this card to your compost.

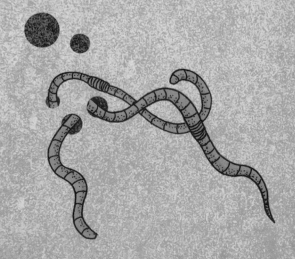

Worms

As well as helping soil, worms do a great job of getting air into your compost heap and moving the material about – potentially saving you the job of turning (see page 34). They tend to work more in a cool heap (this is the type that you add compost to gradually rather than building it all in one go). There is one type of worm that is vital to a certain type of compost-making called 'vermicomposting'.

Springtails

There are lots of springtails in compost. These tiny, wingless insects munch up some of the smaller bits including grains, pollen and even nematodes. They jump when surprised (which is where they get their name from) so you can sometimes see them when you take the lid off a compost bin.

Slugs and snails

You don't often hear gardeners calling slugs or snails friends, but in the case of a compost heap, they can be good at tackling some of the tougher material. The ones you find in the heap often prefer eating dead plants rather than our lettuces. If they lay eggs in the compost, these eggs will most likely be eaten by a predator or killed as you spread the compost on the garden.

As well as all these creatures that eat the organic matter, there are lots more that create a web of life within the compost heap. For instance, beetles, centipedes and ants will eat many of the organisms mentioned above. This is just another example of compost helping to increase **biodiversity** in your garden.

SPRINGTAILS

WORMY FACT
Much of the planet is becoming less biodiverse as farming becomes more intensive, so the more we can do to help in our gardens, the better.

SLUGS & SNAILS

Luscious leftovers

Do you eat everything that is put on your plate? Are you sure? Even Brussels sprouts? However good you are at eating, there are always some bits of food that are left over. Fancy chewing on a tough cabbage stalk, or a satsuma skin? No, I didn't think so.

Don't waste it

Do you know what happens to those bits of food if you just throw them in your bin? They get taken to landfill sites where the rubbish takes ages to rot. And these big holes in the ground fill up and then we have to dig up more land to fill with more rubbish.

Let's find out more

Fruit and vegetables come from plants, but we only eat a small amount of those plants. Potatoes get peeled, apples get cored, pumpkins are deseeded. Although people don't eat these waste bits, they contain lots of good nutrients that other animals can use.

Who will eat it?

You could feed it to a pig… But only if your bathroom is big enough to keep a pig in! Luckily, the tiny little guys we met on pages 15 and 24 are already in your garden, waiting for you to build a compost heap. When you do, they'll be able to live and eat there – it will be their house and restaurant all at the same time!

OOPS

Heaps of compost

So, not only is making compost good for plants, it also reduces waste and is good for the planet! As well as your leftover fruit and veg, there are other things from your house that usually get put in your rubbish bin, which you can use to make compost instead. If you have a pet gerbil, for example, instead of putting its dirty bedding in the bin, this makes great compost!

ALL THE THINGS ON THE LIST HERE CAN BE COMPOSTED

Mmm, there's not much for me to eat around here!

We're just vegging out.

WHAT CAN YOU COMPOST?

FROM THE KITCHEN:
* Tea bags and leaves, coffee grounds
* Egg shells
* Raw fruit and veg leftovers
* Cardboard – toilet roll, egg boxes
* Newspaper or shredded paper – yes, you could even compost this book!

FROM THE GARDEN:
* Grass cuttings
* Weeds – try not to put in perennial weeds or ones with lot of seeds
* Prunings and hedge clippings
* Old house plants
* Leaves

OTHER THINGS:
* Urine (see page 40)
* Used animal bedding – gerbil, hamster, rabbit, etc.
* Manure
* Wood ash
* Human, dog or cat hair

A compost menu

The stuff that you think is horrible mouldy leftovers would seem like a tasty buffet to a worm. Let's take a look at the menu in the gourmet worm restaurant. You might shudder – slimy old vegetables? Rotten old fruit? But to worms, this menu sounds perfectly delicious!

Of course, worms won't really need a menu like the one opposite – that's just for fun. They're happy to eat their food all mixed up. And they don't even need plates, or knives and forks. If you've got the right food for them, worm dining is really, really simple.

I've heard the food here is really rotten.

Yes, it's covered in mould – just how I like it!

WORMY FACT
It takes hundreds of years to make just a couple of centimetres of soil.

CAN I COMPOST IT?

COMPOSTS SLOWLY... YES!

GRASS CUTTINGS, WEEDS, PLANT CLIPPINGS

WOOD ASH

CUT HAIR, PET FUR, NAIL CLIPPINGS

HORSE OR COW MANURE

MEAT, FISH, OR DAIRY PRODUCTS

AVOCADO STONES (bashed)

WOODY PRUNINGS (cut up small)

FALLEN LEAVES & OLD PLANTS

HAMSTER OR RABBIT BEDDING

RAW VEG & NON-CITRUS FRUIT

EGG SHELLS (crushed)

CAT & DOG POOP

COOKED FOOD (e.g. rice, bread, etc.)

TEA BAGS & COFFEE GROUNDS

CITRUS PEEL

CARDBOARD & PAPER

Menu

APPETIZERS

Brown cardboard, moistened with old-tea-bag juice
Apple cores wrapped in potato peelings with rotten tomato sauce
Extra-tough broccoli stalks, served up with some carrot tops

STARTERS

Soup of the day: coffee and carrot with eggshell pieces
Avocado skins stuffed with onion skins and rotten strawberries
Brown salad: slimy lettuce, with a special aged juice as a strong and unusual dressing

MAINS

Vegetable Special: congealed mixed vegetables
Fennel filo (for the worm connoisseur!): slivers of fennel stalk and leaf steeped in a compost jus and wrapped in seven layers of crisp onion skin
Brussels sprouts (customer favourite!): served up in a really big pile

DESSERT

Citrus peel Special: only in small quantities! (Too much citrus will give your worms indigestion and unbalance your compost)
Rhubarb compote aged for three weeks, then chopped into a textured brown mush
Fruit salad special – the mouldy fruit from the bowl
See the board for daily specials

COFFEE & TEA

Served all together...

Hot heap or cold compost?

So now you know what worms and their friends like eating, but how, and where, do you serve this big bug-based banquet? Should you get a compost bin, and if so which type? Let's have a look at the two main composting processes – hot and cold – and some of the compost bins that are available.

Hot composting

This needs lots of good organic material and is the best method if there are big piles of woody stuff and grass cuttings in your garden, as you can build a heap in layers, all in one go. It heats up from the activity of the organisms inside working to break down the material – just like you get hot if you run around! This heat helps to make compost quickly and can even kill off weed seeds.

Cold composting

This is the most common method. It takes a bit longer than hot composting, but is perfect if you have a small garden, or only compost your kitchen waste. Just add the material to the top of the bin or heap, and the worms and other compost friends will do their work!

INSIDE A COMPOST BIN Here you can see the freshly added kitchen scraps at the top, and lovely dark brown finished compost at the bottom!

WORMY FACT
If you have space, it is best to have two bins or heaps, so you can let one finish while putting the fresh material into the second one.

Composting on soil

Compost bins are designed to hold together the organic material while the composting process – hot or cold – takes place. Most sit on the soil, letting organisms climb into the heap to do their work (if you put it on paving it can take them a bit longer to get in). With many designs, you put the compostable material in the top and take the finished compost from a door at the bottom.

Composting away from soil

Some compost bins don't need a soil base and can even be used in the home.
Table-top composters let you make compost even if you don't have a garden! They are like a mini version of an outdoors compost bin. Some use electricity to aerate and turn the compost, to copy what happens in a bigger hot heap. Most have a tap at the bottom to drain off liquid, which is a great plant food!
Tumblers – a hot composting design for outside that lets you turn (or 'tumble') the compost while it's inside the bin. This lets lots of oxygen into the compost, which helps it break down quickly. You often have to add water to these to keep the compost moist enough.

WOODEN COMPOST BIN
A simple design that sits on the soil. Organic matter is added through a lid in the top.

TUMBLER This keeps compost away from the soil, and the design allows for the compost to be easily turned.

KEW-MUNGOUS COMPOST!

Kew Gardens in London makes 4,000 cubic metres of compost each year, using its own green waste, and manure from the Royal Artillery horses. This humungous hot heap warms up to 140°F (60°c) and has to be damped down to stop it spontaneously combusting. It rots down in just eight weeks!

How to build a compost heap

For all the ready-made compost bins you can choose from, there's nothing wrong with an old-fashioned home-made compost heap! The materials are cheap, it's easy to build, and it's a fun family activity.

WHAT YOU WILL NEED

4 STRONG, WOODEN POSTS (at least 1.8m long and 5cm diameter or square)

3 OR 4 WOODEN PALLETS of the same size. It doesn't matter what size they are as long as they are all the same. If you can't find pallets you can use bits of plank or other wood instead.

NAILS, ROPE OR STRONG STRING to fix the pallets to the posts – the nails need to go through the pallet and into the post so should be at least 7.5cm long.

✷ Chicken-wire netting
✷ Staples ✷ Straw
✷ A convenient place to put your heap!

1 Choose a place for your heap to live, then mark out a square – each side should be the same length as the pallets (or other wood) you use. It doesn't matter too much if it's not exactly square, but you don't want there to be any gaps between the posts and the pallets.

My new home! Just what the Compost Doctor ordered.

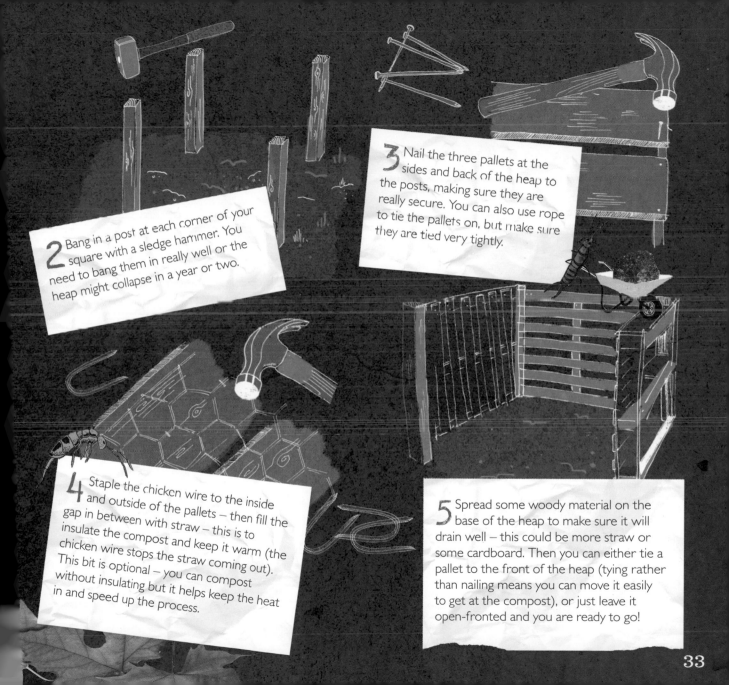

2 Bang in a post at each corner of your square with a sledge hammer. You need to bang them in really well or the heap might collapse in a year or two.

3 Nail the three pallets at the sides and back of the heap to the posts, making sure they are really secure. You can also use rope to tie the pallets on, but make sure they are tied very tightly.

4 Staple the chicken wire to the inside and outside of the pallets – then fill the gap in between with straw – this is to insulate the compost and keep it warm (the chicken wire stops the straw coming out). This bit is optional – you can compost without insulating but it helps keep the heat in and speed up the process.

5 Spread some woody material on the base of the heap to make sure it will drain well – this could be more straw or some cardboard. Then you can either tie a pallet to the front of the heap (tying rather than nailing means you can move it easily to get at the compost), or just leave it open-fronted and you are ready to go!

Caring for compost

Whichever method of composting you choose, there are things you can do to help your compost thrive. Cold heaps and bins are fairly easy to manage (though we have some tips), so we'll start by looking at what you can do to make your hot heap or bin a success.

Helping a hot heap

The most important thing to get right is the balance of elements called carbon and nitrogen. Nitrogen gives compost short-term energy, starting the composting process. Carbon gives the compost long-term structure, stopping it from becoming too wet. All compostable materials contain different amounts of these. Colour is a good guide to how much of each there is – browner items (such as cardboard) contain more carbon, while greener materials (such as grass cuttings) have higher nitrogen. As a rough guide, you want about 30 carbon bits to one bit of nitrogen, but don't worry about getting it exactly right. If you have lots of very green material, like grass clippings, then a small amount of a very high carbon source like cardboard will balance it well.

Turning

Hot heaps need turning to stop them becoming too hot. If you have a spare heap or bin, you can move all of the material from one to the other. If you only have one, you can fork it all out and then put it back in. This helps get air in, helping the microorganisms, and lets you add extra stuff if you think it is too wet or too dry. How often your compost needs turning depends on how hot it is – it will need turning regularly during the hot phase (see opposite).

A green feast for the eyes!

Although we don't have any...

34

Temperature phases

1. WARM PHASE
This phase starts as soon as your layered material is added. If you get the ingredients right, it will quickly heat up further until...

2. HOT PHASE
This is when most of the work is done by the microorganisms. The centre of a heap will always be the hottest, but turning helps to make sure that the edge bits get composted too, and stops it getting too hot for the microorganisms to work!

3. MATURING PHASE
This is the final and longest phase where your compost cools down enough for the worms to move in and finish off the work. Once they're finished, you have compost!

If everything goes perfectly you can make good compost in just eight weeks, but it is more likely to take anything from six months up to a year. The more you look after it by turning and checking if it's too dry or wet then the quicker it will be.

FEELING HOT HOT HOT

TEMPERATURE

160°F (71°C)
140°F (60°C)
120°F (49°C)
100°F (38°C)
80°F (27°C)
60°F (15°C)
00

WORMY FACT
Worm eggs can survive in compost or soil for as long as 15 years.

Mmm, this is delicious! And not too hot! Dig in, guys.

Caring for cold compost

Cold composting relies on organisms that prefer cooler temperatures, such as worms, to break down your organic matter. The timing and contents of the heap are less important than with hot composting, but it's still good to keep an eye on how it is doing. Over time, the material in a cold heap or bin will break down even if you have a bit too much of one or the other, but keeping a good balance of layers, and turning it every so often, will help it happen more quickly.

This method takes longer than hot composting and doesn't kill things like weed seeds, but is still a great and simple method.

Seasonal changes

The things you have available to put into your compost heap will vary from season to season. Veg scraps will be coming out of the kitchen all the time, but you won't get any grass cuttings in winter, and you might get lots of woody material when big winter jobs are being done, like cutting back plants or hedges. The best way of dealing with this, if you have the space, is to pile up the woodier material (shredded or chipped if possible) to add to the heap gradually over the summer when there is more green stuff.

Wood can also be burnt (we all like a good bonfire!) and the cold ash added to the compost. While the ash is good for compost because it is very high in potassium, most of the carbon from the wood will be lost in the air, which means you won't get the benefit of it for your garden. Also it's not great for the environment as it contributes to high carbon dioxide levels. If you don't have room in your garden to store material, you could look for a green waste recycling scheme, or join a community composting scheme – see page 44.

WORMS & LADDERS

Can you climb your way to the top of the heap, or will the hungry worms beat you to it?

WHAT YOU WILL NEED

To play Worms & Ladders, you will need dice, and a counter for each player. Your counter could be anything that fits on one square of the board – you could use a bottle top before you recycle it, or perhaps a coin.

HOW TO PLAY

1 Starting on square number 1, the aim is to be the first player to reach 'home' – the top of the compost heap in square 64.

2 Roll the dice to begin the game. The player who rolls the highest number moves their counter onto the board first.

3 Take turns to roll the dice and move up the board following the numbers in sequence.

4 If your counter lands on a square at the bottom of a ladder, you can 'climb' up it and move your counter to the top. If your counter lands on a square with a worm's head in it (that's the top end!), your counter must slide down the worm to the square its tail is in.

5 To win the game you need to roll the correct number to land on square 64.

Layering

The perfect heap should have alternating layers of brown and green material, for a good balance of carbon and nitrogen (see page 34). Here are some of the things you can put in each layer...

DARK BROWN LAYERS
Carbon-rich material. Usually (but not always) the thinnest layers: cardboard, newspaper, wood chip...

LIGHTER BROWN LAYERS
Leaves, straw, tomato plants that have died back, sweetcorn husks...

LIGHT GREEN LAYERS
Kitchen waste, weeds (don't include the seeds, though!), horse manure...

DARK GREEN LAYERS
Nitrogen-rich material. Chicken manure, cut grass...

Compost doctor

So you've read the book, chosen a bin or built a heap, lovingly layered it, and despite doing everything right, your compost isn't working properly. It's time to speak to the compost doctor...

Q Why are there rats in my compost?
A Your heap needs to go on a vegan, gluten-free diet! There is no sure way of getting rid of rats, and they eat pretty much anything, but they do prefer things like meat, cheese and bread, so don't put these on the heap. They also prefer not to be disturbed, so regular turning will help deter them, and should certainly prevent them making their nest in the compost.

My compost always rots down at a snail's pace!

WORMY FACT
Worms may survive being frozen if they don't freeze too quickly.

Q Why is my compost dry and dusty?
A Are you putting lots of woody material into the heap? Try to find more green stuff like grass cuttings, or shred the woody stuff separately and compost that bit first, then add to your main compost once the fungi have started to work on it. Sprinkling with water occasionally helps, but you still need that nitrogen-rich material to really get it going.

Q Why is my compost cold and slimy?
A Compost can get too wet if you only add very green material such as grass cuttings and kitchen waste. Cover your heap (with a bit of old carpet or a wooden cover) to keep it drier, turn it to get air in, and add brown material like plain cardboard, shredded plain paper, woodchip or leaf mould to help dry it out.

Q Why are there no worms in my compost?

A Well-made hot compost has no worms in it, so don't worry as they should come in during the maturing phase. If your cold compost heap on soil has no worms, it might be too dry or too wet – try the remedies for these problems and you should get the worms racing back!

Now things are cooling down, I'll worm my way back in.

Q Why are there some bits of food that haven't rotted?

A If you find that things like eggshells, avocado stones and Brussels sprout stalks won't rot down, then try to break them up as small as possible before adding to the heap. Crush up egg shells, bash avocado stones with a hammer and, if possible, cut tough stalks into smaller bits. When you come to put your compost on the garden, if there are bits that haven't broken down, just put them back in the heap – they will eventually compost!

Q Why is my compost so slinky?!

A Often composts that have got too wet will smell either of wee or just a bit 'rotten' like old eggs. With no air, the good bacteria can't work and the smelly ones take over. This usually means the pile has too much green material or is too wet (or both). You need to do the same as for a wet heap and add some nice brown, carbon-rich material.

Q Why does my compost heap have flies?

A This should only happen for a short time and usually happens when you put fresh kitchen waste at the top of the heap or if you add meat or cheese (which generally shouldn't go in the heap at all). If you get flies, just turn the heap a few times and it should sort the problem out.

Activators & additives

Over the years, many people have looked for ways to speed up composting and make better compost by adding a whole range of ingredients. Here are some of the things that are said to help…

Activators

Activators are things that kick your compost into action. Usually they contain food for the microorganisms that do the work, but some contain the microorganisms themselves! The cheapest activator is your own finished compost as it already has all the organisms you need – just add some of it to your new compost mix. You can also try:

• **QUICK-RETURN COMPOSTING** This involves adding layers of a mixture of natural ingredients such as nettle, dandelion, chamomile, oak bark and honey through the compost heap. You can buy this as an additive or make your own recipe.

BOKASHI This Japanese system uses bran that has had good bacteria and yeast added to it, to dry out and break down the material you want to compost. Once it has begun the process, you then add the half-composted

material to your normal compost heap. It even makes cooked waste, meat and dairy products compostable. You can buy Bokashi bran in garden centres and online.

Weeeeeeee!

Urine is very high in nitrogen, so is a great activator. You can go directly on the heap if you're tall enough (check with an adult first!), or collect it in the house and dilute with water to make it go further. This works really well if you have a lot of woody material that is difficult to compost.

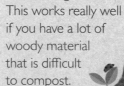

Weeeee

Additives

These do not necessarily speed up the process, but aim to improve the quality of the compost you make, either by adding extra nutrients or improving the way that the compost structure works.

ROCK DUST Made from ground-up volcanic rock, this contains a huge range of minerals and nutrients, which can sometimes be missing in soils, especially those that have been growing vegetables for a long time. Even if you find it does not accelerate or activate your compost, your heap will love the extra nutrients!

BIOCHAR Biochar is really just charcoal like you might see on a barbecue (usually ground up), but it is made at a lower temperature. This makes it become like a sponge so it can soak up nutrients from the compost heap and then slowly release them for your plants to use once the compost is added to the soil.

CLAY This helps bind compost together, which allows it to hold on to nutrients better. Many traditional compost recipes say you should add a little clay. You can make a nice sludge by mixing some clay and water, and then 'sprinkle' this onto your compost. If you have a clay soil you can just add a bit of soil to your compost as you make it.

WORMY FACT
Earthworms are not female or male, but both. They need another worm to make baby worms.

Compost tea

Before you rush to the kitchen to put the kettle on, compost tea is not something you're going to want to drink! It's called tea because you make it by putting compost into water and 'brewing' it like you would tea, but it's your plants that will enjoy this drink.

What is compost tea?

Compost tea is a liquid that you make by adding good quality compost to water and molasses (a thick dark brown liquid that is produced when sugar is made) or seaweed liquid, and bubbling air through it. The tea contains not only nutrients but also active microorganisms that can help a plant to grow. It's not very hard to make, but you do need some kit to do it properly (see opposite).

How does it work?

As we've seen, there are lots of good bacteria and fungi in well-made compost. Compost tea lets you use these to protect your plants from the bad bacteria and fungi that can cause disease, just like you might eat a live yoghurt to boost the good bacteria in your own digestive system. If there are enough of the good organisms on a leaf or flower then the bad ones find it harder to get in. It works a bit like a neighbourhood watch scheme, where all the residents keep an eye out for people coming in to steal things from their houses.

I do love afternoon compost tea!

WORMY FACT
Charles Darwin played whistles, bassoons and pianos to prove that earthworms are deaf!

Healthy plants

Compost tea is not medicine; it is to stop plants getting ill – like you might take vitamins to stop getting a cold. If it works it will keep your plants strong and healthy.

You can buy ready-made compost tea, or if your compost isn't ready yet but you want to have a go at making tea, you could buy the compost and start from there.

FAMILY ACTIVITY

WHAT YOU NEED to make COMPOST TEA

1 Some really good compost – a badly made or diseased compost will just increase the unwanted bacteria and fungus on your plant.

2 A compost tea maker – you can buy these or make your own simply by putting a small air pump, like the ones used in fish tanks, into a plastic container or bucket.

3 Some molasses and seaweed liquid (available in garden centres) – this helps to feed the organisms that you are trying to breed, giving you greater numbers in a short space of time.

4 Some time – brewing for 24 hours is normally recommended, but it can be done in as little as 12 hours or as much as 3 days, depending on the system and how active you want it to be.

COMPOST TEA MAKING KIT
You can buy ready-made kits such as this one, which includes a container, aerator pump and 'food' to get things started.

What do I do with the tea?

Once you have either made or bought some compost tea, you should spray it onto the soil or the leaves of your plants every week or so. You could use a hand-held water spray or, if you have lots of plants to treat, you can get something bigger from your local garden centre.

Community composting

Now we all know why making compost is important and fun, but how can we make it even more enjoyable? Doing something on your own is good but composting with other people is even better. Here's why!

Why compost with other people?

Bigger heaps get warmer, so everything composts better! Your family may not have enough veg waste to keep a really good compost heap going, but you can contribute your material to a big community heap with other people, getting a better quality compost back at the end of it. Collecting from a range of gardens also means community heaps get a better balance of woody and green material.

It can also help to deal with some of the trickier waste, like big, woody bits. By collecting all the woody stuff together in a big pile, a machine called a chipper can be hired to produce woodchip, which you can either use as **mulch** or add to your compost heaps.

How does it work?

Rather than building a heap in each garden, people in a community bring all their material to one central place to compost. You can take all of your waste there, or you could have a small compost bin at home that you put kitchen scraps in but bring your bulky woody material to the central point.

What do you need to get started?

The two most important things are somewhere to do the composting – this should be a biggish, flat site with access for cars and preferably for bigger vehicles too – and a group of people who want to do it. It's good to have one person who knows how to compost and has some time and lots of energy to help lead the project too.

'Mulch' is any material – organic or otherwise – that you spread around the base of plants to stop weeds growing, and to help keep moisture in. Manure and woodchip are often used as mulches.

WHO CAN HELP?

While all you really need to start a community composting group is some people and a plot of land to compost on, there are some people who can really help you get started and make a success of it.

✳ Community composting organizations have lots of experience of helping groups to start up and avoid some of the things that might go wrong.

✳ Community gardens or allotments are great places to start a community composting system (many will already have one set up).

✳ Local schools are a great place to find other people who might want to compost. How about starting one up in your own school? Perhaps a corner of the school grounds could be used?

✳ Farmers have land and machinery and they, or the local stables, may be able to spare a little manure to add to your compost occasionally.

✳ Tree surgeons sometimes need to get rid of the woodchip they make from cutting down trees. They might also have chipping and shredding machines that you could hire or borrow.

Heroes of compost

So, who are the people and what are the breakthroughs that have helped us to compost better? Here are just a few, but why not do your own research and try to find some more? You may find a local hero who changed the way composting is done in your area.

NATURE Nature has been composting since the beginning of life and, left to its own devices, still knows how to do it best. We still need to find better ways of dealing with the huge quantity of waste that we produce in the modern world.

I'm a compost champion!

COMPOSTING TOILETS Chinese inventors are thought to have invented the first composting toilets around 4,000 years ago! These are now coming back into fashion as a way to recycle precious nutrients that otherwise get flushed out to sea.

GEORGE WASHINGTON 1732–1799 As well as being an American president, George Washington conducted many trials with compost, as he knew how important it was, and he used it to improve the fertility of his farm. He even built a special barn on his land to make really good compost in.

SIR ALBERT HOWARD 1873–1947 Albert Howard studied agriculture at Cambridge University, then went to teach farming in India. He soon realized that he could learn more from his Indian colleagues than he could teach them. He used this knowledge to develop a composting method called the 'Indore' system and other soil management techniques that helped start the organic movement in the UK.

MAY E. BRUCE 1879–1964 Inventor of the quick-return composting method, a writer and farmer and one of the founders of the organic charity The Soil Association.

CLARENCE G. GOLUEKE 1911–2004 The undisputed American composting guru, he lived to the ripe old age of 93. He was a scientist, and a writer on all things compost. In particular he studied how to make the best use of solid human and animal waste through composting.

PROFESSOR MICHAEL RAVIV 1946–PRESENT DAY Having published a textbook and many studies on growing plants out of the soil, his main focus for the last 20 years has been organic agriculture. He is still researching and teaching in Israel on a range of compost and fertility issues, especially using compost to reduce diseases found in the soil.

J. I. RODALE 1898–1971 Originally a playwright and publisher, he was one of the founders of the American organic movement; he 'brought' composting to America and indeed is believed to be the person who gave 'organic' its modern meaning for ecologically produced food. He also founded the Rodale Institute.

DNA TESTING Everyone knows that DNA testing helps to catch criminals and improve disease treatment, but did you also know that it is giving us new techniques for studying compost microbes? As this knowledge grows, our understanding of how compost really works is sure to increase.

We're kings of the heap!

THE FUTURE Your garden could be the place where something amazing is discovered, or even more importantly, you could become the composting hero of your house, your street or your school!

Index

Picture credits

p. 31 Kew compost, Andrew McRobb/ copyright RBG Kew.

p.43 Courtesy of Keep It Simple, Inc. (www.kisorganics.com)

Fotolia: Main book: 8, 16, 22, 31, 40.

istockphoto press-out Worm Lovers' Society card (frame image).

Nature PL: Extras: pull-out worm measuring chart (*Eisenia fetida*; *Octolasion cyaneum*; *Lumbricus terrestris*).

Shutterstock: Main book: 12, 22, 30, 31. Extras: pull-out worm measuring chart (large worm image); stickers.

Kiddish font courtesy of Matt Bruinooge

AUTHOR'S ACKNOWLEDGEMENTS

for

Ivan & Jonah.

Thanks to Ruth for everything, Dad for the love of gardening, Monica, Dan Carpenter for earthworm help, and all of my colleagues at the Soil Association.